FIRST WORDS
100 ANIMALS

Children's Reading & Writing Education Books

Speedy Publishing LLC
40 E. Main St. #1156
Newark, DE 19711
www.speedypublishing.com

First Words
Animals

Bird
Goat
Sheep

Farm Animals

Goat

bird

bull

duck

Dog

Turkey

Elk

cattle

Geese

goose

calf

Donkey

Barn Animals

Pig
Cow
hicken
Rooster
Turkey

sheep

horse

cow

pig

hen

ram

calf

chicken

rooster

turkey

Dolphin
Tunny
Whale
Clownfish
Starfish
Crab

Marine Animals

stingray

tunny

starfish

crab

clownfish

salmon

eel

Tuna

whale

octopus

Shark

dolphin

African Animals

Rhinoceros
Gazelle
Panther
Scorpion

Elephant

Gazelle

Rhinoceros

Lion

Scorpion

Panther

Baboon

Antelope

Lemur

Cheetah

Pangolin

Warthog

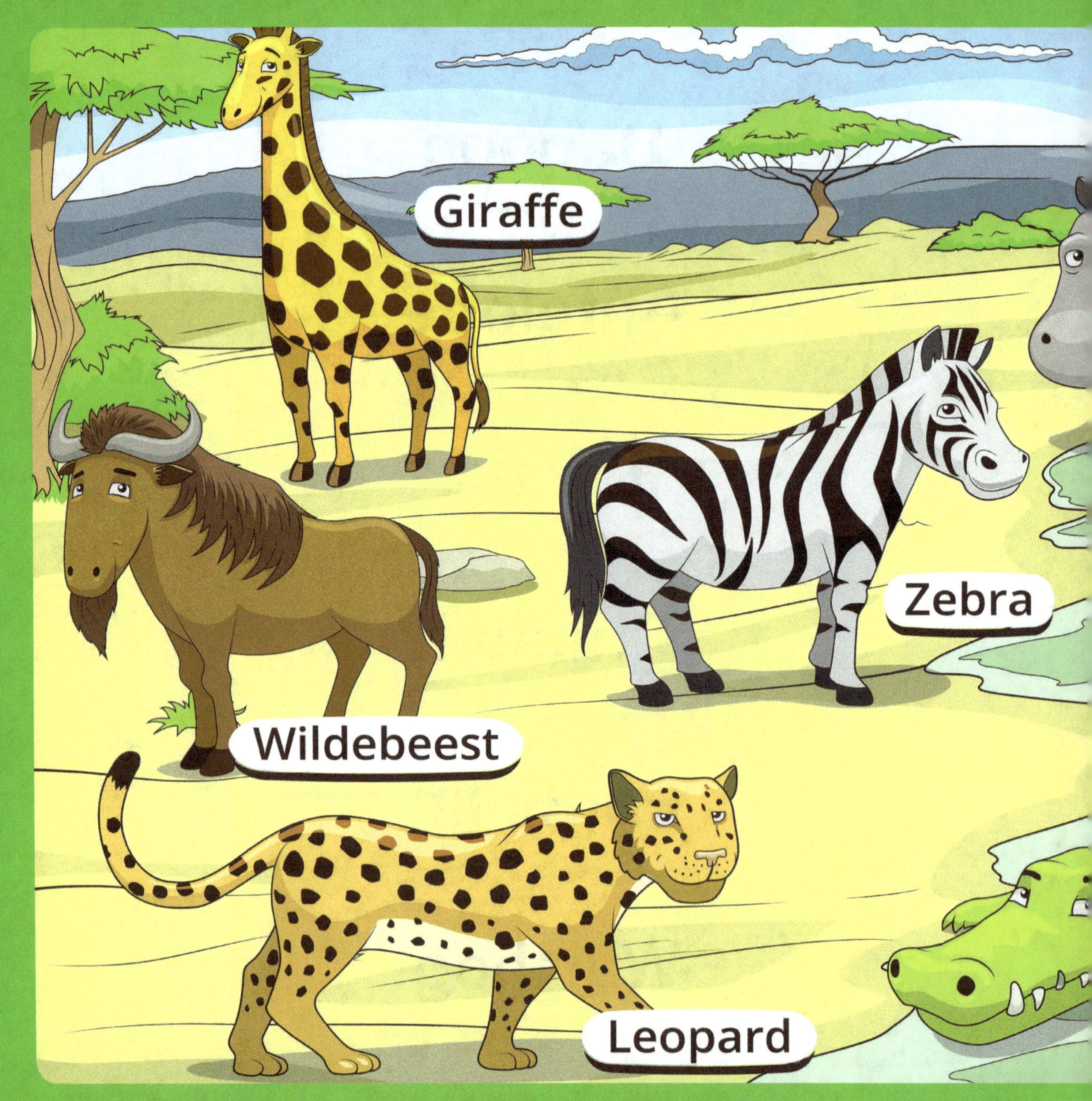
Giraffe
Zebra
Wildebeest
Leopard

African savannah Animals

Giraffe

Zebra

Hippo

Wildebeest

buffalo

Leopard

Ostrich

Crocodile

Hyena

Snake

Underwater Animals

Turtle
ordfish
Jellyfish
ng
Sea Horse
Oyster

sea horse

seal

squid

whale

lobster

shrimp

oyster

octopus

Clam

starfish

Sloth
Boa
Tiger

Jungle Animals

Boa

Sloth

Parrot

Gorilla

Tiger

Frog

Python

Chimpanzee

Skunk

Cobra

peacock

Coyote

Forest Animals

Owl
Roe
Wolf
Hedgehog

Bat

Roe

Fox

Wolf

Woodchunk

Hedgehog

Owl

Beaver

Rabbit

Porcupine

Squirrel
Boar
Bear
Hare

Forest Animals

Bear

Squirrel

Boar

Insects

Deer

Beaver

Hare

Racoon

Eagle

Wolf

Deer

Hummingbird

Visit
BABY PROFESSOR
EDUCATION KIDS
www.BabyProfessorBooks.com
to download Free Baby Professor eBooks
and view our catalog of new and exciting
Children's Books

www.ingramcontent.com/pod-product-compliance
Lightning Source LLC
LaVergne TN
LVHW060511170826
845677LV00026B/1712

* 9 7 9 8 8 6 9 4 4 5 1 3 1 *